TAKING CHARGE OF
YOUR EMOTIONS

GREGORY DICKOW

TABLE OF CONTENTS

EMOTIONS: WE ALL HAVE THEM

~

Chapter One

Emotions—we all have them; unfortunately, there are times when they have us!

Wouldn't you like to get control of them rather than them having control of you? You certainly can. But how? That's what the next few pages of this book are going to show you.

Mastering Life. This whole teaching stems from the revelation that we were designed by God to master life, rather than it mastering us—that we were made in the image of God to reflect His power, His love and His authority in this earth.

It starts in our emotions, or our soul, because God says in 3 John 2 *"Beloved, I wish above all things that thou may prosper and be in health, EVEN AS THY SOUL PROSPERS."* So as your soul goes, the rest of your life follows.

God created us to be in control as He is. However, in our failure to control our own self, we attempt to control others, in an effort to feel the superiority that God created us to have. Though perhaps currently displaced, it is God's will for us to get back on top in this life—to reign in this life.

Mastering your emotions doesn't mean not having emotions. God designed us to express passion and emotion; but sin, the devil and the curse have perverted these emotions so that they will hurt us and hurt others around us.

Men, Women and Emotions. While women identify with this subject easily, this is by no stretch of the imagination for women only. The fact is, women are blessed to be more aware of their emotions (as your husband may attest, if you are married!)

Men have as many emotions as women. We need to get rid of the notion that women show their emotion more than men. The fact is, they show *different* emotions than men, but not more—perhaps simply more recognizable.

Women have more of a tendency to be expressive outwardly of their emotions; whereas men have more of a tendency to internalize their emotions and bury them. Now, a woman might have an outburst of her emotions verbally, but a man's outburst of emotions might be a grunt or a sigh.

The Sand Box. Have you ever noticed little boys and girls playing? Perhaps you even remember playing in a sand box. A girl will be talking in the sandbox, saying something like: "Look at my beautiful castle, little boy! See the flag that I put on top? That's where the princess is going to sleep and this down here is where the front door is... and this over here is where the water goes all around the castle... Hey! Watch out! This is my river... don't mess it up!"

What is the boy's response? He grabs a truck and goes "vroom, vroom, mmm, mmm, mmm, mmm, mmmm."

Then the little girl taps her friend and says, "Little boy, are you listening to me?" And he responds, "Hmmm?" He hardly talks! But he's bothered by her interruption, nonetheless! Girls learn to vocalize themselves a whole lot earlier than boys do. Some boys never learn to express themselves but they're always good at grunting!

When we grow up, a wife says, "What do you want for dinner tonight honey?" Husband's response: "mmhmm" (Translation: "I don't know.")

Wife: "Well, I was thinking about making spaghetti. Would that interest you?" "Mmhmm." (Translation: "fine with me!")

Men express themselves differently than women, but both men and women, when they are not born again, are under the curse of being controlled by their emotions. As believers, we are redeemed from this curse; however, we need to learn how to walk out of being "emotionally ruled" people.

The "C" Word: Control. The word "control" is one of the most misunderstood words in our culture. It usually has negative connotations.

There has been a lot of Christian and secular writing that condemns the idea of a "controlling" personality. And rightly so, as it usually describes insecure people trying to control others in order to feel powerful or feel value.

People that try to control others are people who cannot control themselves—and usually this is found in the failure to control our emotions. We'll deal more with this later, but it's important for us to deal with the root causes of our problems at the onset so we can truly be free.

We all need to feel we are in control. There is nothing necessarily wrong with being in control. The issue is: what are we supposed to be in control of? When we get a hold of our thoughts, then we'll have control of our emotions. When we get a hold of our emotions, we will have peace and security on the inside, eliminating our need to control others.

I want to show you that if you can control your emotions, you can absolutely do anything! Proverbs 16:32 says, *"Better is a man who can rule his spirit (emotions, attitudes) than one who can capture a city."* Look at how powerful a person actually is who can control or "master" his emotions. He is more powerful than an army that takes a city!

In contrast, the person who is under the control of his emotions is like a person overtaken by an army.

But God made us to be in control—or better said: to walk in our authority.

- You can take control of your emotions.

- Self-control is a godly force designed by God to direct our lives where He has designed them to go.

- Uncontrolled and unyielded emotions lead to controlling the wrong thing: people.

In this book, I want to share with you the importance of taking charge of your emotions; the root cause of negative emotions; and a simple guide to dealing with the most common emotions in our lives.

Jesus Had Them Too

Chapter Two

What are Emotions? Emotions are feelings on the inside caused by pain or pleasure trying to move us in a certain direction. Jesus had emotions, yet His emotions did not have Him! There were times, however, where He was tempted, as we are, yet without sin (Hebrews 4:15).

In Mark 14, Jesus was struck with emotion when He was preparing to go to the cross. Verse 33 says He felt "terror and amazement," and was "deeply troubled and depressed." He said to His disciples in verse 34, *"My soul is exceedingly sad so that it almost kills me!"* What an amazing picture of some of the emotions that each one of us face.

But what did Jesus do about them? He did not allow them to determine His decisions. He knew God wanted Him to go to the cross, but His feelings tried to move Him in a different direction. Verse 35 says, *"He went forward and kept praying."*

While our emotions will often try to influence and determine the decisions we make, we must do what Jesus did:

1. He went forward. Keep going in the direction you know God wants you to go, no matter how you feel.

2. He kept praying. Talk to God when you feel "struck" with emotion, fear, discouragement or depression. Pray through it!

How we deal with our emotions will determine whether we experience the blessing or the curse in life. The ultimate curse that came into the world when Adam sinned was the curse of being an "emotionally ruled" person. This doesn't mean it's a curse to "have emotions." We just need to make sure they don't "have us!"

Reasons for Taking Charge of Emotions. Let's look at a practical example. Let's say a person gets excited about the financial potential of a product or a stock like many did years ago with the dot-com craze. As a result, they decide to invest because of their excitement, rather than sound principles and the leading of God. Their "emotional decision" ends up being a mistake and they lose all or most of their money. This happens all the time, not just in our finances, but in many areas of life. We are all tempted to be swept away by the feelings that come from the "appearance" of a thing, rather than the substance of it.

As with Adam and Eve, something may look good to the eye (Genesis 3:6). It looks like it will make one wise and appeals to the physical or emotional appetite or need, but it can kill. That's what I mean by "the curse of being emotionally ruled."

In fact, there ought to be a number of factors in making quality and successful decisions (rather than emotional decisions):

1. *Accurate knowledge (Hosea 4:6).*

2. *Wisdom or wise counsel (Proverbs).* The best counsel comes from God's Word; additionally, I would consult with people who have succeeded in the area that I am considering.

3. *Understanding the process necessary to achieve the desired goal.* If it's a great marriage you are after, for example, you should obtain understanding of the process, or the simple steps (well, maybe not so simple)—to obtaining that desired marriage.

Many problems in your marriage, finances and health are related to emotions. The 1994 earthquake in Northridge, California shows us the emotion of fear affects our physical bodies. Three times as many people as usual died of heart-related conditions on the day of that earthquake according to a study done at Good Samaritan Hospital (New England Journal of Medicine 2/96).

Emotions can play a major role in releasing chemicals causing depression, anxiety, stress, leading to physical sickness, disease, or a chemical imbalance.

Emotions are the source of sin in our lives. Once we're born again, we're freed from the power of sin; but to the degree we gain control of our emotions, to that degree we will walk free from sin's dictates.

The blood of Jesus defeated the devil, but it did not defeat our flesh. We have to control our flesh, and emotions abide in our flesh; therefore, we must control our emotions.

GET TO THE ROOT

Chapter Three

A Sense of Powerlessness. This is the root of every negative emotion in our lives—a sense of powerlessness. If you want to stop the fruit of a bad temper, anger toward yourself, resulting in depression and condemnation, you have to deal with the root. Incidentally, depression is simply anger turned inward, which produces condemnation and a feeling of hopelessness. All of these patterns of negative emotions stem from the root of powerlessness—feeling that you cannot change.

There are several things that the devil tries to tell us that we cannot change:

- Our circumstances

- Our personality

- Our weaknesses

You have a God-given right to change these things in your life. What is the extent of our God-given authority? First we must get a brief understanding of world history.

God gave authority over the earth to Adam in the Garden of Eden. By sinning and listening to the serpent, Adam gave his authority to the devil.

When Jesus came to the earth, 1 John 3:8 tells us He came to destroy the works of the devil! Almost everybody understands that Jesus died for our sins. And although He obviously did, His greater purpose was to take back the authority that man had lost. That's why He came to the earth as a man—to get back the authority over life, death, and the earth—that Satan had obtained from Adam. Through His death and resurrection, Jesus regained that authority (Revelation 1:18).

That's why Jesus is called the second Adam—the second lord of the earth—Adam being the first...

After Jesus took that authority, He gave it to every born-again believer who calls on His name (Matthew 28:18; Luke 10:19; Acts 1:8). This is where our power and authority come from.

When we understand the power God has given us, we will eliminate the sense of powerlessness that causes negative emotions.

What will release this power in your life?

Know Who You Are. In Acts 19:13-16 we see the story of seven young men attempting to cast the devil out of a man. They are quoted as saying to the demon, "we adjure you in the name of Jesus who Paul preaches, to come out of this man."

The demon responded, "I know Jesus, and I know Paul, but who are you?" This resulted in the demon leaping on to these seven young men and attacking them!

The point here is that the devil had access into the lives of these men because they didn't know who they were. Since *they* didn't know who they themselves were, the devil didn't know who they were either.

When you know who are, you become dangerous to the devil. As a believer, you have authority and dominion. You are restored to the image and likeness of God. The knowledge of "who you are in Christ" releases the power of God in your life.

This is the first thing the devil challenged in Adam and Eve in the garden. This was also the first thing the devil tried to challenge when he tempted Jesus. *"If you are the Son of God, command these stones to be turned into bread,"* (Matthew 4:3).

Jesus knew who He was. He was able to overcome and resist all temptation because He knew who He was. He never said to the devil, "Yes, I am. I am really the Son of God."

He didn't need to do that because He knew who He was. If Jesus would have had an "identity crisis," He would have been tempted to do things in order to gain approval or prove Himself.

God took care of that in Mark 1:11, when He told Jesus, after His baptism, *"You are my beloved Son, in You I am well pleased."*

You see, God affirmed Jesus and established His identity before He performed one miracle. By doing so, God was saying, "There's nothing You have to do to earn Your identity.

You are what I said you are, and nothing can change that. There's nothing You can add to it, and there's nothing You can take away from it."

And so this is true for you as well. You cannot add to "who you are." That's why we are called, "human beings", not "human doings."

'Who you are' is what empowers you to do what God has called you to do.

So who are you?

- **You are a son or daughter of God!**
  (John 1:12).

- **You are a joint heir with Jesus Christ!**
  (Romans 8:16).

- **You are the seed of Abraham!**
  (Galatians 3:29).

- *You are the righteousness of God!
  (Romans 5:17; 2 Corinthians 5:21).*

- *You are more than a conqueror!
  (Romans 8:37).*

- *You are a king and a priest before God! (Revelation 1:5-6).*

As you understand these descriptions of you, you will begin to walk in the power of the **REAL YOU!**

Now, let's talk about some of the major emotions each of us deal with and how to be free!

REJECTION

Chapter Four

Rejection is the feeling that you are not loved, not accepted, or not good enough for God or for others. It's the feeling that you don't belong; or that you are not included by those whose association you desire.

It also is the feeling that you are unwanted, unimportant, and not valuable. It is the sinking feeling of walking into a room knowing that you don't look good enough, have enough money, or position. It's that feeling that everyone is better than you. It leads right into low self-esteem.

You may say, "Pastor Dickow, where did you get this definition from?"

From growing up in it! I wish I could tell you how great it was to grow up in a loving home, where affection and acceptance abounded. But I can't. I had to overcome much rejection growing up. Being Middle Eastern, and looking different from everyone else, was difficult in the white suburbia that we grew up in. Being ridiculed, called names like "camel-jockey", which is funny today, but hurt then, among other things—gave the spirit of rejection its foothold in my life.

My parents did not neglect our material needs. They did what they knew. But they knew little about our spiritual or emotional needs. The real need in a child's life is acceptance, affection, love, strong discipline accompanied with tight hugs and lots of kisses—and most of all a real relationship with God.

Children need to see their parents kissing, hugging, loving each other. The absence of this in the home leads to feelings of rejection, especially if your parents were divorced, which is true in 50-60% of homes.

Of course, a divorce in the home is always preceded with lots of yelling, name calling, and, in many cases, unfaithfulness. This further alienates a child and makes him feel guilt and more rejection. He or she lives their life trying to be loved, trying to be accepted. This is typically what leads girls to look for love in pre-marital sex. This typically leads guys to drugs, or gangs. A gang provides a perverted sense of acceptance and covenant love. While there are many who didn't need a bad upbringing to lead them to sin, a godly upbringing can sure do wonders.

We all have a story, we have all had it tough; but that's irrelevant if you know how to recover.

How I got free from rejection:

1. I got born again and realized that I was a new person. The feelings of rejection didn't leave right away but their power over me was destroyed.

2. I found out what it meant to be the righteousness of God. It meant that I was His son, His prize, the apple of His eye. It meant that I would never be rejected again and never be lonely again. The first thing we ever hear God say to Jesus is, *"You are My Beloved, Son. In You, I am well-pleased."* It's amazing that He said that to Him before He did one sign, one wonder, or one miracle. He said it to Him after He had "fulfilled all righteousness." (For Jesus, He fulfilled all righteousness when He was baptized. For us, we fulfill all righteousness when we are born again.) I believe God told Him that so that we would know that our acceptance from God is not based on

our works or how spiritual we are; how we look or how much money we have; but by being His righteousness. You are loved, and you are His!

3. I forgave my parents and everyone else who ever hurt me. Nobody may have meant it, but it happened. Again, there are those who may laugh at their past, but have you dealt with it once and for all? Or has it left a scar so deep that you have grown accustomed to it? There are many people who know the deep pain that comes from rejection. And this step by step process will deliver you. You can be free!

4. I stopped being the villain in everyone else's drama and the victim in my own. You can't control what other people think about you or say about you, so stop worrying about it. You really don't need to be accepted by others, you need to know you are accepted by God. You need to know that if God is for

you, who can be against you? It really won't matter when you know God is on your side.

5. I started finding others who hurt more than I did and reached out to them, accepted them, and prayed for them. The Scripture says, *"associate with the lowly."* Something happens when you reach out to someone else who is hurting.

6. I broke free from co-dependency on people. I love people and admire people but I don't need people. Neither do you. God is your source. See people as an opportunity for you to bless, not as someone you need anything from.

SELF DOUBT

Chapter Five

Self-doubt is questioning ourselves all the time. It is feel-ing guilty all the time—feeling like when you are praying, you should be reading your Bible. When you're reading your Bible you feel you should be praying. It's feeling like when you are sleeping, you should be up getting things done; feeling like when you are married, you should be single, when you're single, you should probably be married. It's thinking that when you are black you wish you were white; when you're white, you wish you were black. It's feeling like you prayed, but it's not going to work. You've confessed your sin, but you still feel guilt; feeling like you haven't done enough for God, for your family, for the world. Self-doubt is really being double-minded. And James 1:7-8 says that the double-minded man cannot receive anything from God; and a double minded man is unstable in all his ways.

Self-doubt is a demonic attack against your self-worth, your self-esteem, and your confidence.

Why is it so dangerous to lose your confidence? Because 1 John 3:23, and 1 John 5:14-15 say that when we have confidence before God, we will always receive the answer to our prayer!

Again, what gives us confidence is not what we have done for God, but what He has done for us. Stop doubting yourself! How?

1. Believe the love God has for you. 1 John 4:16. You have more value than you realize! Think about this for a moment. How do you determine the value or worth of something? Well, go into an art museum and look at some of the most expensive pieces of art. They often are the ugliest pieces! Some of the paintings look like someone just threw a can of paint up on the canvas. Yet people will pay millions of dollars for those pieces.

Why? Because the value of a thing is not determined by what something looks like or how much it cost to make; but it is determined by how much someone is willing to pay for that thing.

Your worth, and your value don't come from your looks or your talents. Your worth comes from how much God was willing to pay in order to have you as His own!

If you weren't valuable to God, He wouldn't have spent so much to have you! He paid for you with the life of His own Son. There wasn't enough money in the world to purchase you; not enough jewels, not enough gold, not enough of anything. So God bought you with His own blood!

You have value, you have worth.

You are precious!

2. Stop second guessing yourself. Do what God tells you to do. Peter started walking on the water, and then he looked around and SAW the wind, and became afraid. He second-guessed, he doubted himself, and he hesitated. As a result, he sank!

3. Stop condemning yourself. Instead of listening to every condemning thought in your mind, speak to those thoughts. The way you take a thought captive (2 Corinthians 10:5) is with something greater than a thought—words. Say to that thought, "I resist you in the name of Jesus. God loves me, I am not condemned and I cannot fail. God is on my side!"

CONDEMNATION

Chapter Six

Condemnation can be so discouraging. We feel like we're not good enough. We feel like we don't do enough. We feel we can't become everything God wants us to be. We feel defeated because of a sin or a mistake from our past. These are some of the ways condemnation affects people.

You cannot build upon a faulty foundation. If you do things because you are condemned and you are trying to rid yourself of it, then you will never be free. You have to see that condemnation, guilt and fear are the most hideous forces in the universe. They work their way into our soul and sit at the base of our lives as tyrants. When you make a decision because of guilt, condemnation or fear, they have become your master.

How do you stop condemning yourself?

1. Realize God never condemns you. (John 3:17, John 8:7-11).

2. If you've blown it, confess it. God cleanses you from every sin. (1 John 1:9).

3. Accept God's mercy, which is new every morning! (Lamentations 3:22).

4. Realize He is still working on you. Philippians 1:6 says, "Faithful is He who began the good work in you. He will finish it."

FEAR

Chapter Seven

Here is the granddaddy of them all. This was what caused Adam and Eve to sin in the first place. In fact, this was the first sin. It wasn't the sin of eating what they shouldn't have eaten. It was the fear that God was holding something back from them. It was the fear of not having enough. It was the fear that they were missing out on something. This came from the devil. He is the one who is really missing out. He is the one who is never going to have enough. He is the one that can't be like God. Adam and Eve were already like God! The devil is such a liar. He is always trying to tell us we don't have something that we really do have.

All fear is rooted in the fear that God's Word won't work. Fear of poverty is really the fear that Philippians 4:19 *(God shall supply all your need…)* won't work.

Fear of sickness is really the fear that 1 Peter 2:24 won't work or isn't true. *(With His stripes, we were healed.)*

Our decisions should be based on what pleases God; on what God has said. We should never allow fear and condemnation to motivate us.

Many have thought that fear is a good motivator, but it is a lie. It may look like you can get immediate results when you are motivated by fear, when, in reality, it digs its heels deeper into your soul and before you know it, it becomes the most natural response in your life.

A woman could be afraid she will not be accepted or loved, so she does everything she can to make herself look beautiful. There is nothing wrong with doing what you can to look beautiful, but it should be motivated out of a healthy love for yourself, rather than the fear that you aren't good enough.

A man can be afraid that he is not going to be popular or happy unless he is rich enough or successful enough. So his fear motivates him to excel; his fear motivates him to do better.

Many would say, "But look at the result. It worked for him." But it can work properly if he says, "I want to be pleasing to God. I want to succeed so that the world will know how good God is. I want to be blessed so I can be a blessing to everyone I come in contact with."

The difference is the motivation. If what we want is motivated out of the fear that we won't have enough, or that we are going to be left out, then that fear will torment us.

Furthermore, God said in James 4:2-3 *"You ask and receive not, because you ask with the wrong motive."*

The "motive" here is the wrong "motivation." When fear is our motivation, we will not receive from God.

God is moved by faith, not fear. We need to be motivated by faith, rather than by fear. Fear can be motivating us without us even knowing it.

It is often ingrained in our thinking. That's why the Bible says we are to take every thought captive to the obedience of Christ. Every thought that comes into our head should be judged. We should ask—is this thought "fear based" or "faith based"? If it is "fear based," then we need to change our mind. That's what repentance is—to change our mind.

We would be wise to look at our motives, not to condemn ourselves, but to see what is behind the decisions that we make. If fear is behind it, it will eventually lead to defeat and destruction. If faith is behind it, it will lead to success. Most of all though, it will be pleasing to God.

Fear brings torment.

Faith brings victory!

How do we get free from fear?

1. Know God's love. Perfect love (God's love) casts out all fear (1 John 4:18).

2. Most fear comes from not knowing what's going to happen. Well, the Bible says in John 16:13 that the Holy Spirit will reveal to us the things to come. So if we can know what's going to happen, there is nothing to be afraid of.

3. Fear also comes from feeling powerless over the future. Most people think that whatever is supposed to happen is going to happen. This is false teaching. This stems from the idea that God is in

control over everything. And while that sounds comforting, it's not true. He has given us control over many things, including our future. How can we control our future? By the seeds we sow. Whatever we sow is what we are going to reap, so as we sow the seed of God's Word, then we can know, exactly, what we are going to reap.

4. Live by faith. Fear is the opposite of faith. Faith comes from hearing the Word of God, and fear comes from hearing the words of the devil or words of doubt. Decide to listen only to God's Words.

Again, I want to reiterate how important it is to stop second-guessing yourself. The Bible calls this being "double-minded." When we are double-minded, James says, *"we cannot receive anything from the Lord."*

This is where Adam and Eve stumbled. They questioned whether they really were made in the image of God. Satan got them to think that they needed to eat from the tree of knowledge in order to become like God, something they already were!

And so are you! You are made in the image of God. You already have His power available to you when you are born again. You need not doubt yourself or God when you know who you are!

ANGER

Chapter Eight

Who has never been angry? Here is an example of an emotion completely rooted in the need to control or manipulate. You can be free from anger!

Again, the key is to get to the root of a thing, and then we can stop the fruit of it.

I have heard many people give so many reasons why they get angry. They're Italian, they're Irish, they're Puerto Rican...our nationality, our color, our sex—none of these are the reasons we get angry; and none of these are reasons we get emotional.

There is nothing wrong with having emotions; it's when they have you that there is a problem. Anger is one of those that can come on so suddenly and do such damage in such a little time.

James 1:19 gives us some insight as to the root of anger. In fact, God gives us a step-by-step process. Let's look at it and see how to experience total freedom from anger.

"Be quick to hear; slow to speak and slow to anger; for the anger of man does not achieve the righteousness of God."

1. *Be quick to hear.* Often we get angry because we have misunderstood something. Certainly there are other reasons we flare up, but we are wise to follow James' advice. It's important to understand that God gave us two ears and one mouth. That means we're supposed to listen at least twice as much as we talk. It's interesting to notice how many times when we're in a conversation that we are not even listening to

what the other person is saying. We are thinking of what we are planning to say next. This would go a long way in our marriages, with our children, with business and mostly with our relationship with God. Listen clearly before speaking!

2. **Be slow to speak.** Everything begins with our mouth—everything good and everything bad. How many times have you wanted to take something back that you have said, but those words were too far out of your reach the moment you said them? Our words set the course of our life. They are like the match that can start a forest fire. A very famous passage of Scripture makes it very clear—*Death and life are in the power of the tongue.* Proverbs 18:21. If you want to be free from anger, slow down. Be in a hurry to listen and act like a turtle before you speak. Sl-o-o-o-w down and think twice

before you speak. You may say, 'But I'm not like that. I can't control my mouth. It's my best way to communicate.' Well, that's where you're wrong. You do have control of your tongue and the devil wants you to think you don't. Stop making excuses why you can't keep you're mouth shut. It works for you at night! As Kenneth Copeland put it years ago, "Learn the vocabulary of silence."

3. ***Be slow to anger.*** Here is how it works: If you follow step #1 and #2, this will come much easier. It's a process. As you are quick to listen, you will be slower to speak. As you are slow to speak, you will be slow to anger.

But the Scripture goes on to give us another key to being free from anger. It says, "For the anger of man does not achieve the righteousness of God."

I would like to zero in on those words "anger does not achieve." This is the real reason we get angry—we think it will achieve something. We think that it produces something. And we're right, it does produce something. But we don't want what it produces—strife, hatred, retaliation, stress, sickness, and so much more.

Since anger cannot achieve righteousness, why get angry?

I don't know about you, but when I buy something and discover that it doesn't work, or doesn't produce what I thought it could, I stop using it or I take it back. Once you realize that anger will not bring the results that you thought it would, you will stop using it.

MANIPULATION

Chapter Nine

There are many people who do use anger to get things done; however, it is manipulation. If you have to make someone feel guilty to get them to do what you think they should do, you are manipulating them. Whatever immediate results you get, you will eventually lose. If you have to use anger to get someone to hear or understand you, again, you are using manipulation and it will eventually backfire.

God calls this witchcraft in Galatians 5:19-21, and it is known as the work of the flesh. It's not even a spiritual force, but it is a force of the flesh. It uses the flesh's power to get things to change. That's what witchcraft is—a demonic substitute for spiritual power. Instead of using the Word and the fruit of the spirit to change something, we use the flesh—anger, hatred, manipulation, guilt, etc. These works produce death, not life. And whatever results we get from them won't last.

When we recognize how ineffective the works of the flesh are, we will break the cycle of operating in them.

Don't get discouraged. You may be reading this and saying, "I understand the importance of being free from anger and manipulation, but I have a real struggle with this. I don't know if I can change and I don't know how."

Remember, it's that sense of powerlessness that is the root to negative emotions. You have the power to change. Jesus gave you that authority, and as you focus and learn more about who you are in Christ, that is what releases the power of God in your life to change. I'll explain more about what kind of power you have in the next chapter.

JEALOUSY

Chapter Ten

Jealousy is to feel discontent because of what someone else has. Jealousy is also to view someone else's success as a threat to your own success.

Consequences of Jealousy

1. **It causes you to lose hope.** Jealousy causes hopelessness and depression (Proverbs 23:17-18).

2. **It makes you cruel** *(Song of Solomon 8:6)*. Proverbs 27:4 shows us a progression. "Wrath is bad, anger worse (like a flood), and jealousy the worst (you can't stand)".

3. ***It causes you to have limited power.*** According to 2 Corinthians 10:12, when we compare ourselves, we are without understanding. 1 Corinthians 3:3 says, "For since there is jealousy and strife among you, are you not fleshly and are you not walking like mere men?" God has not called us to be mere men.

4. ***It brings bitterness*** *(James 3:14).*

5. ***It brings confusion.*** James 3:16 says, "Where jealousy is, there is disorder and uncertainty."

Origin of Jealousy

Jealousy, while obviously from the devil, comes from:

1. ***Feeling our needs will not be met.***

2. ***Doubting our own worth to succeed.***

3. ***Feeling a sense of powerlessness.*** This causes you to become jealous of those who have power.

4. ***Insecurity will make you jealous.*** It will make you think you're unworthy so you'll withdraw because you think you can't reach your potential.

How to Be Free from Jealousy: Realize the power you have.

1. ***You have the power of the Holy Spirit.***
    (Acts 1:8—*dunamis*). Romans 8:11 says the same Spirit that raised Jesus from the dead lives in you.

2. ***You have power over the enemy.*** Luke 10:19 says, "Nothing shall harm you." Someone else's success can't hurt you, either.

3. ***You have power over oppressive emotions.***
    (Acts 10:38). By the Holy Spirit and His anointing you have power over all oppression.

4. ***You have the power to get wealth.***
    Deuteronomy 8:18 says, "It is He that gives you the power to get wealth." If you have that, why would

you ever compare yourself with others? You have this power inside of you. Therefore, why be jealous?

5. **You have the power of seed.** Trust in the power of your seed—because if there is something you don't have, you're only a seed away according to Galatians 6:7.

The Power of Contentment. Being content is a valuable lesson to learn here. Contentment is not an acceptance of a low lot in life or the tolerance that things have to stay the way they are, nor is it settling for less than all that God has promised . . . Rather, contentment is the confidence that God is your source and therefore you don't need what anyone else has.

In Philippians 4:11-19, Paul talks about contentment, and declares that God provides all our needs, according to His riches and glory. In other words, when you trust God as your provider, you will be content, and you will sense the peace that comes from it.

The reason Paul was content in whatever state he was in, was because he learned THE SECRET of contentment. It was that he could do all things through Christ. All of the treasures of wisdom and knowledge are in Christ. All of our riches are in Him. All of our security is in Him. All of our blessings are in Him. When you are IN CHRIST, you have access to everything. You lack nothing! For, in Him, you have found the secret to life. That is real power!

DEPRESSION

≈≋≋⌐

Chapter Eleven

If you are dealing with depression, first, remember that Christ has redeemed you from the curse of the law. You are redeemed from being emotionally ruled.

Realize God loves you and is personally interested in you. He has invited you to His table—to dine with Him (Revelation 3:20). Go to Him. Many people think that they have to be special in order to come to Him; but it's the exact opposite. You become special by coming to Him!

Depression is a result of external pressure getting inside our heart and weighing it down. Stress and pressure internalized, lead to depression. The feelings of depression come from thinking thoughts that weigh you down. You will have to change the way you think if you want to change the way you feel. Let's follow some simple steps out of depression:

1. *You must watch over your heart.* John 14:1 says, *"Let not your heart be troubled, you believe in God, believe also in Me."* You have control over whether or not you allow your heart to be troubled—based on what you believe. Believe in God; believe what He says and depression will lose its grip.

Proverbs 4:20-24 says to watch over your heart with all diligence for out of it flows the issues of life. You are not always in control of your circumstances, but you are always in control of your heart. You have to choose not to allow the circumstance into your heart. What we choose to believe is what determines what we allow into our hearts. Depression cannot stay if you are holding on to God's Word and His promises.

If you allow the trouble around you to get inside you, its seed will produce a harvest. Therefore you must make a decision to not let your heart be troubled. How?

2. Speak to your problem, rather than speaking about your problem. Mark 11:23 says, *"Whosoever shall say to this mountain, be thou removed and does not doubt in his heart . . . he shall have whatsoever he says."* This is a one-way conversation you must have with depression and the things weighing down your heart. Speak to it, not about it.

3. Next, if there is something missing in your life, ask God for it. In John 16:24, Jesus says, *"Ask and you shall receive, that your joy may be made full."* He gives us a key to being free from depression: Receive what you ask for and joy will come. How do you receive? Believe you have whatever you ask for, whether you feel it or whether you don't. Faith says, "I got it." "It might not look like it, but I got it."

4. Then thank Him. Praise Him. Praise rebukes depression. You can't stay depressed very long, if you start praising God. Praise Him for what? For saving you, loving you, forgiving you, and accepting you. The list can go on and on if you start thinking on what He has done for you. Make a list. Go over it again and again. You will not be able to stay depressed, as you keep thanking Him.

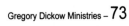

STRESS

Chapter Twelve

Dealing a Death Blow to Stress. We must recognize stress as an enemy. Proverbs 1:17 says, *"Surely in vain, the net is spread in the sight of any bird."* If you put a net up in front of a bird, he's going to fly around it, over it, or turn around and go the other direction. He sees his enemy and he avoids it.

The devil has set a net for us—he disguises himself as an angel of light. When we know how he operates, we can avoid his trap. Stress is an enemy. Let's look at some of its fruit.

Some signs of stress are: forgetfulness, temper, chronic fatigue, cynicism, sense of helplessness, never having a sense of accomplishment, feeling like a failure; constant illness, headaches, tension, migraines, high blood pressure, and heart disease.

Stress is often the root cause of these symptoms, and we have learned we must deal with the root if we want to stop the fruit.

The fact is, we will have trouble at times. 2 Corinthians 4:8 says, *"We're troubled on every side, but not distressed."* Just because we have trouble, does not mean we have to have stress. It doesn't have to affect you or force you to make a decision that you would not have otherwise made. Be prepared for trouble by knowing how to respond before it comes.

First and foremost, don't panic. Psalm 34:19 says, *"Many are the afflictions of the righteous, but the Lord delivers him out of them all."* Even though trouble comes, deliverance always comes! We need to know God always provides a way of escape. Trust Him.

Causes of Stress.

1. ***Uncertainty.*** Take control of the seeds you're sowing, and you can be certain of the harvest you'll get. The Scriptures give us absolute certainty about how things are going to turn out in our lives. Having certainty delivers us from stress.

2. ***Unresolved Conflict.*** Resolve it fast. Be at peace with all men as much as it has to do with you. Don't let the sun go down on your anger. (Ephesians 4:26)

3. ***Unrealistic Comparisons.*** Don't compare yourself to other people. Saul began to have problems when he compared himself to David,

resulting in stress and anger. 2 Corinthians 10:12 says you'll be without understanding when you compare yourself with others.

4, *Unconfessed Sin.* Confess your sin to God. He cleanses you from all unrighteousness.
(1 John 1:9; James 5:16; Psalm 32:3). When you bury sin, it buries you!

5. *Unusual Pressure In the Area of Finances.* Stop spending more than you earn. Meditate on things that are more valuable than money – the Word of God; wisdom and understanding; the anointing. Give. Sow seeds. He who gives to the poor lends to the Lord (Proverbs 19:17), and God pays back with interest! Get a financial plan. A lack of order causes stress.

Some Practical Ways to Be Free:

1. **Stop trying to remember everything.** Write things down.

2. **Stop trying to please everybody.** Please God. Live by faith!

3. **Take care of your body.** Get rest. Exercise, eat healthy and get to know how your body works so you can take care of it properly.

4. **Stop jump-starting your body** with false energy such as coffee and sugar.

5. **Talk to your problems** rather than about them.

God's Solution to Stress (Philippians 4:6-8):

"Be anxious for nothing, but in everything by prayer, with supplication and thanksgiving, make your requests known to God. And the peace of God which passes all understanding shall keep your hearts and

your minds through Christ Jesus. Whatsoever things are true, honest, just, pure, lovely, of good report . . . think on these things."

We often think how important it is to eat right for health purposes. And while I agree with the importance of eating the right foods, I want to emphasize the greater importance of thinking the right thoughts, which causes the right emotions. Though an improper diet can be a leading cause of sickness in our bodies, an improper response to life's problems can often be a greater cause of sickness in our bodies.

And so we need to give as much attention to being emotionally healthy as we do to being physically healthy. We may realize how wrong it is to eat unhealthy foods, while giving no thought to the bad attitude we have towards somebody, or the unforgiveness we have towards someone. That unforgiveness and attitude can hurt you more than that box of donuts!

Take Charge Now!

Chapter Thirteen

If you can rule your emotions you can rule your life. When you master your emotions, you will make right decisions—and decisions are the stuff life is made of. You will be happier and freer than you have ever been before.

When you master your emotions, you release supernatural power in your everyday life. When you master your emotions, your faith is unlimited.

Your husband or wife will be glad you did. You'll be glad you did.

If you can take charge of your emotions, you literally have the power to do anything!

All emotions in essence are working against your ability to believe what God says. The force of fear, worry, anxiety, depression, anger, etc. are all designed by the devil and by our flesh to derail our faith. They attempt to move us in a direction other than God's will.

Since all things are possible to him that believes (Mark 9:23), the devil wants nothing more than to get you focused on what you feel and what you see, so he can limit your ability to believe God's promises.

Faith works based on what is not seen. Emotions work based on what is seen.

Furthermore, the man or woman who conquers himself, cannot be conquered. Remember Proverbs 16:32 . . . Rule your self; rule a city!

The curse of sin is

"to be an emotionally ruled person."

Negative emotions do not destroy a life. But when not dealt with properly, they lead to bad decisions; and bad decisions ruin a life.

Emotions start with a thought. So get control of your thoughts and you can have complete control of your emotions.

You were created by God to master life, to reign in life. You were not meant to be pushed around by life and its circumstances. Through God's abundant grace and His gift called righteousness, you can reign as a king in this life (Romans 5:17 AMP).

God put you in control over your thoughts, your feelings, your life. Our failure and unwillingness to get control of our self is what leads to the abusive attempts to control and manipulate others.

The fruit of the spirit is "self control." Not "spouse control" or "others" control.

Negative emotions do not just run in your family. They run in all of our families! But through Jesus Christ, you can begin again. *"If any man be in Christ, he is a new creation."* (2 Corinthians 5:17). You are a new creation with a new power . . . the power to rule yourself . . . the power to rule your future. Start today! How? Very simply:

1. ***Realize that the array of negative emotions that we feel do not have the power to bring to us what they falsely promise***. For example, anger does not bring relief. Lust does not fulfill your true desires. Fear does not prepare you for anything.

2. ***Reverse the curse.*** A thought becomes an action. An action becomes a habit. A habit becomes your character. Your character becomes your destiny.

3. ***Start with your thoughts.*** Every emotion has a root thought. Emotions are a direct harvest of whatever we are continually thinking about. Picture a registration desk in your mind. Every thought that desires to take up space in your head has to check in at the registration desk. If that thought is not a thought of peace, victory, confidence, etc. do not let it register. Don't let it in.

4. ***You overcome negative thoughts with words.*** If you begin to feel depressed, say out of your mouth, "I'm the happiest person in the world. I'll never be depressed another day in my life." The force of your words is greater than you may realize. And your

thought life will be shaped by the words that come out of your mouth. Your emotions will then take the shape of your thoughts. Your decisions will follow. And your life will get better and better.

5. **If you blow it, don't sweat it.** Don't condemn yourself. Sometimes the devil doesn't need to condemn us because we are capable of doing a pretty good job of it ourselves. If you sin in your emotions, confess it to God. The blood of Jesus cleanses you and changes you.

6. **Know that you can change.** God is not finished with you. He began a GOOD work in you, and He will complete it (Philippians 1:6).

7. **Use this book as a practical guide for victorious living.** When you're struggling in an area, go back to that section. Follow the steps. Meditate on the verses given.

Don't give into the feelings that tell you to quit or tell you, "You're not going to make it; you'll never change, you can't win."

You can win! In fact you have already won. Romans 8:37 says, *"You are more than a conqueror."*

2 Corinthians 2:14 says, *"Thanks be to God who always leads us in His triumph…"*

God is your Father. He's not mad at you. He's mad about you! He loves you. He believes in you. In fact, He believes in you, more than you believe in yourself! If you ever feel like giving up, realize that God never gives up on you. He is on your side. He began a good work in you; and He will complete it.

About the Author

Gregory Dickow is the host of "Changing Your Life," a dynamic television show seen throughout the world, reaching a potential half a billion households. He is also the founder and Senior Pastor of Life Changers International Church, a diverse and thriving congregation in the Chicago area with several thousand in weekly attendance.

Known for his ability to communicate the power and principles of God's Word clearly and concisely, Pastor Dickow lives to see the lives of people dramatically changed forever.

Pastor Dickow is also the host of "Ask the Pastor" a live radio show reaching the world through radio and the internet with live callers asking hard-hitting questions about their real-life problems. Pastor Dickow is reaching people personally, encouraging them and empowering them to succeed in every area of life.

Other Books Available by Pastor Gregory Dickow

- Acquiring Beauty
- Breaking the Power of Inferiority
- Conquering Your Flesh
- Financial Freedom
- How to Hear the Voice of God
- How to Never Be Hurt Again
- Taking Charge of Your Emotions
- The Power to Change Anything
- Winning the Battle of the Mind

Audio Series available by Pastor Gregory Dickow

- Financial Freedom: Strategies for a Blessed Life
- How to Pray & Get Results
- Love Thyself
- Mastering Your Emotions
- Redeemed from the Curse
- The Blood Covenant
- Building Your Marriage God's Way

You can order these and many other life-changing materials by calling toll-free 1-888-438-5433.

For more information about Gregory Dickow Ministries and a free product catalog, please visit *www.changinglives.org*